HOLY TOLEDO!

John Clegg was born in Chester in 1986 and grew up in
Cambridge. In 2013 he won an Eric Gregory Award. He works
as a bookseller in London.

John Clegg

HOLY TOLEDO!

To Lindsay
with my best wishes
27/09/16

[signature]

Cambridge

CARCANET

for Jo and Bill

First published in Great Britain in 2016 by
Carcanet Press Limited
Alliance House, 30 Cross Street
Manchester, M2 7AQ
www.carcanet.co.uk

Text copyright © John Clegg 2016

A CIP catalogue record for this book is
available from the British Library,
ISBN 9781784102609

The publisher acknowledges financial
assistance from Arts Council England.

CONTENTS

Socorro	09
The Lasso	10
The Great Tradition	11
Zorro in the Bear Republic	12
Fly Lab	14
Lacklight	15
Figtree	16
Tenaya Overwintered in Yosemite	17
Duet	18
Holy Toledo	19
Signal	20
Heroes of Arventine	21
From the Journals of Don Diego de Vargas	22
An Offer of Service	23
Roadkill Ocelot	24
A Translation of 'The Andalusian Fountains'	25
Real Stories: A B-Side	26
Bloomsbury	28
New Bearings	29
Larval Midgut	30
Shelving	31
Socorro	32
The Long 1850s	33
The Warren Commision	35
The Common Pursuit	36
Candidates	37
Milton's God	39
Donald Davie in Nashville	40
Ramsonde	41
High Table	42
Yvor Winters and Buffy Summers	43
In a DARPA Lab	45

Firewatching   46

Two Birds   47

Guatavita   48

For the Old Cavendish Laboratories   49

Rain Bird   50

A Blended Index   51

T for Texas   52

What Grows, and Some Divisions   53

The Signal and the Noise   55

Revaluation   56

The Field Goal   57

Peach Tree   58

Notes   61

Acknowledgements   62

'But then again outside, scarcely a hundred steps before this incomparable city, it should be conceivable to meet a lion on one of the unconcealed paths and make him beholden to one by something quite unintentional in one's bearing.'

Rainer Maria Rilke, letter to
Princess Marie von Thurn-und-Taxis Hohenlohe
Toledo, All Souls' Day 1912

SOCORRO

Stumbling over that fabled city –
some Piro Indians, sat in a loose circle.
One offered water, another
the group's first and only
deliberate gesture:
then salt crystals on the horizon
dissolved and refocused:
Teypana pueblo, its lowslung adobe,
its flood precautions.
In the desert it was the god Thirst
our four-bead rosary told and told,
red, white, red, white, last white the moon.
Salt still fogging the blood
as we hammered the stakes home
        for succour, Socorro.

THE LASSO

That I had time to think, *I still have time*
not to correct my grip but drop the rope
before the lasso fell and yanked away
the loop I'd somehow nocked around my thumb.

That I had time to notice I could think
and that the time to think in was reserved
for thought, like hours in a monastery.
I knew, because I saw and still held on.

That I had time, time sinking like the rope
around the moment's neck, and I had thought
like slackness in the rope, the little loop
that half a moment's tension would wrench true.

That I had time and then the time was taut.
My thumb, erratic firework, shot past,
and in the time reserved for me to breathe
I swear my wrung hand tightened on the rope.

THE GREAT TRADITION

I followed every wire in the server room
once, waiting for the photocopier-
cum-scanner to flog through another
thousand pages, hitchless, you could
hear the all-clear subsong. My job
was to stand in that cool air and unjam
stuck sheets. This was Cambridge
and the server room was former Kings
accommodation, reaching through
the racks your hand brushed marble
sunflower bosses on the fireplace,
I pinched the inside wire, keeping track
and thought of Heather, could her book
be really on *The British-Irish Lyric*
as a whole or was I misremembering?
Two wires seemed to have no terminus.

ZORRO IN THE BEAR REPUBLIC

Meadow needs backstory.
This is grassland
being put to scythe,
its third or second
season under man.
And path needs more
than bent grass,
boot marks, landmarks.
This is like the single-use
way tracked by ships.

Here country
puts aside its name
for stretches.
On an outcrop rests
the mower's jacket,
pocketed whetstone
and flask in shade.
He mows
erratically
the inexhaustible.

If asked
(who'd ask?)
his guess at where he lived
would be dependent
on the speed of news.
One night the land
secedes by fiat,
two weeks later
reattaches like cloud
to a different country,

Easterly
and overheavy now.
Meanwhile at what will never be a real
ford, a river
only named on maps
is peeling back
the foil from the gold.
The mower breaks
since time out here's
like space,

divisible by whim.
He nibbles
at the bark teat
of his lukewarm
waterskin, pulls off his boots
to number (each
red dot a famous victory
for Mexico)
the numberless
mosquito pocks.

He needs backstory.
One night
on the oldest rancho,
while the Dons
were stringing fishline
marking tract
and cattle-right on land
they'd never seen,
possession terms
on places not yet properly yoked

there came a rider
dressed in black

The fly is a scribe.
Its copy-text
is the unimagined idea of itself.
The flask is a cloister.

Actually the whole lab is the cloister.
A. at her microscope
is the monk. The fly
is her marginal addendum.

The microscope is a jeweller's loupe.
The flies are gemstones.
A. is shining them up
with the superfine tip of a paintbrush.

The lab is a factory
for turning flies into ink.
The rate is a thousand flies
per published word.[1]

The flies are a pie of font
with serif bristles.
The microscope is a typewriter.
This is the index.

The fly is a colophon to its DNA.
This is the colophon.
This is an embryo fly
in dazzling false colour, wriggling off the confocal.

[1] Sawala, Annick. Personal communication. 13/09/15

LACKLIGHT

At first we didn't call the dark 'the dark';
we saw it as a kind of ersatz light,
a soupy substitute which shucked the hems
and wrinkles from our objects. That was nice.

And later on we came to love the dark
for what it really was – admired how
(unlike a candle) it could fill a room,
(unlike a torch) it focused everywhere,

(unlike a streetlight) it undid the moths,
(unlike a porchlight) anywhere was home,
(unlike a star) it couldn't be our scale.
In utter darkness we were halfway down.

Then came the age of lacklight, loss of measure,
darkness turned inside to cast a darkness
on itself. Though 'age' would make it finite.
Perhaps we're stuck there, straining in the lacklight.

Still, across the last however long,
I've noticed something budding, vaguely sensed
a nerve untie and reconnect itself.
I think my lacklight eye is almost open.

FIGTREE

He trepans with the blunt
screwdriver on his penknife:
unripe figs require the touch
of air on flesh to sweeten.
Blind, but in his fingertips
he has the whole knot
of this figtree memorised.

The five-inch scar, a vague
felt mesh of parallelogram,
was where he bandaged up
a split branch once.
He starts from there,
first handheight fruit
and then he gets the ladder.

Gauge weight, turn, unturn.
He sings beneath his breath
about the excellence of figs,
their mellowness,
their skin-dints
like the perfect undulation
in the small of his wife's back.

TENAYA OVERWINTERED IN YOSEMITE

Acorns under earth a year
leach bitterness and blacken,
go well raw or roasted.

Our hotel
resorts to Davy lamps.
The bar taps and the TVs stop.

Ground acorns steep in boiled water.
This is changed each day.
They're edible when it runs clear.

The snow is doorframe-deep.
All loans of snowshoes, snow shovels and skis
require a credit card deposit.

Acorn bread is wrapped in amole leaf
then placed among
an 'oven' of hot stones.

All vehicles without tyre chains
will not be towed.
You must return for them in spring.

DUET

The expedition's jinx, breaker of vacuum jars
and laptop hinges, near whom
every drillbit sheared
and every ice core rose contaminated with brown kerosene
and every guyline was a trip hazard,

who threw precision widgets on the fritz
merely by walking past them,
in whose presence the supply plane
overshot the runway – twice – and when unloading
dropped the kilo jar of honey, August's luxury –

that schmuck – secured his funding for another year.
There's barley vodka chilling
in the ice-cairn. On the iPod something slow and sad
does battle with the katabatic wind
the battery-life of all our kit gets drained by.

HOLY TOLEDO

Was it *somewhere near Salinas* Kris let Bobby
slip away, or *somewhere miscellaneous*?

Oxford '61, say – Kris watched Auden lecture,
boxed for Merton, carpooled with the young Morse.

On the train to Carmen's party, A. explained
why *undead* was an oxymoron.

*I pulled my harpoon out of my dirty red
bandanna* – was that Kris's word for *harp*

(harmonica) or *hypo*?
Not a trade name, though the first

harmonicas were marketed as *aeolians*.
Sing, breeze, blow it soft against the river –

as Auden bungs a notebook in the Cherwell,
as a frogman rises with the Saxon buckle,

as the punt squirms, Kris blinks, Bobby vanishes –
as Carmen butterflies into the Thames

off Port Meadow,
the smoulder finds the fringe of kindling

beneath our scrappy bbq, and kicks in
like the drums on 'Shipwrecked in the Eighties'.

SIGNAL

Her tracking microchip's
a rhythmic prickle,
blossoming
into a migraine
after thunderstorms

or when the herd slips under
the invisible
circumference
of a cellphone tower
posing as a bristlecone.

HEROES OF ARVENTINE

Moss DMs
An owlbear
Out of nowhere
Roll initiative

Rockrose
In an imaginary valley
Moss DMs
Reroll initiative

An owlbear
Out of loneliness
DMs its own
Encounter

Rolls initiative
Against itself
A lady wizard
Waiting on a plateau

Moss DMs
Dice crackle
In the cup
Her turn expires

Roll initiative
The owlbear
Crackles
In the rockrose

I mounted on horseback, and with a few military officers
and the Captains Francisco Lucero de Godoy and Roque Madrid,
went to inspect the chapel or hermitage
which was used as a parish church
by the Mexican Indians living in this *villa*
under the title of the invocation
of their patron, the Archangel San Michael:
and having made the inspection, though small in dimensions
and not sufficient for the accommodation of a great number

nevertheless, on account of said
inclemency of the weather and the urgent necessity
for a church in which might be celebrated
the Divine Office and Holy Sacrifice of the Mass,
recognised that it would be expedient and proper
to roof said walls
and whitewash and repair its skylights;
said parties alluded to being present,
and said governors of the aforesaid pueblos, Josèph and Antonio Bolsas,

I commanded that they should send natives
having made measurements in respect of timbers,
and having offered them axes and mules for its prompt transportation
that those who were accustomed to hewing said timbers might do so,
and that those who were fit for the mason's trade
in repairing said walls
should be ordered in like manner, and that I
on my part would have the Spaniards whom I had with me
assist me thereat.

AN OFFER OF SERVICE

Tipped embers skitter down the frozen Cam.
A porter peels back his glove to blow in it.
The moon rides low above the Cavendish
on Free School Lane, and Treason, inconceivable
Elizabethan stage machinery, is stalking
through the empty Hall (a glass pops
on the draining board), through Whewell's Court
and through Blunt's dream: the absolutely
even path down to the water, walled
farm-fort reflected in unruffled calm:
an offer, that was how it hung, deliberately
out of reach. (Ice grates against the Backs.)
As Treason passes through Poussin's foreground
he doesn't scare the goats, he barely dents the lake.

ROADKILL OCELOT

Hard to imagine
sleek except where she's
been drawn back
to the sleek bone.

Scuzzy, says the daughter
of the man who stopped
to see what we
were standing round.

It fits the mottle:
working camo
scuzzying her outline
must have been what killed her.

Microbiome
of the blown gut
shimmers, overblooming
on the tarmac.

Her expression
fluctuates, depending
on the angle
which you read it from.

The narrowest surprise
conceivable
shades into (are you
sure?) this sudden, massive joy.

Stalk pedantically among the thick
cork forest of the copy text – it's tone
which flummoxes; the lynx
that almost sprung the camera trap
slunk off, and in this weirdly Englished
Ibn Hamdis *Lions people the official wood.*

As well they might. Proofreading
someone's hurtling thesis
where they had 'port pilferer'
I made it 'harbour lowlife', saw
the joy recede as sense ebbed in.
It's that I worry at, and find I can't correct.

REAL STORIES: A B-SIDE

for Gareth Reeves

What was it that they'd sprayed the citrus with,
those twelve formation cropdusters?

The radio advised a wet towel in the windowframe.
Police trucks loudhailered through Berkeley *Stay indoors.*

He didn't stop to ask but held one breath
down forty miles of freeway into Davis,

fog encrusted underneath his windscreenwiper blade,
a brittle salmon froth, and in the wheelrims.

The thrips kicked on the orange trees
and may have satisfactorily popped.

Some poems he was writing
have that thrip kick bit, acutely insect scutter:

our talk (aeons later) swung round
to their strange distracted blurb from Szirtes,

'full of sharp discreet vignettes
that mount like evidence' – or had it been *discrete*?

To me that first book's drawn-out California.
Anecdote is contour

somewhere one's not been.
Thrip-blind, we hug our leaf and burrow in and in.

What was the name of that insecticide?
Six syllables put by, the one breath

held for forty years
until the wind changed?

BLOOMSBURY

G. S. Fraser grousing about Empson's voice,
'odd, sad, snarly, rising now and again
to a very high pitch, the Cambridge voice
of the 1920s' – Bloomsbury's run-out groove.

Ten minutes late for work, I listen
to a string quartet tune up in someone's
living room on Thornhaugh Street.
Nearby, the architecture bows and scrapes,

The University of London here
expresses its sincere regret for this extension,
undertaken without the permission or the knowledge
of the Russell Family, who at no stage were consulted –

When Woolf says that *human nature*
changed completely in December 1910
I distrust her, but maybe it changed twice.
The violin, sad, snarled, uncurls its Cambridge voice.

NEW BEARINGS

Djinns trapped inside a mirage
they are waiting for the gods to reinhabit,

which will turn this
rampart dissipating in the rump of noon

to solid crystal.
Here the only factual crenellations

are the castle-caravans
of lizard armour. Creak and drag.

Here even dunes creak,
and the lizard uses this to navigate.

The dune-creak is the note
djinn squawks to djinn, its fizzy maydays half made-out.

They squawk at you in case you are the gods returning.
It is night now you must navigate.

LARVAL MIDGUT

(Drosophila melanogaster)

This is the long way through the fly.
The shortest route is via A.'s
incision down the body wall,
hinging the larva, which adheres
to glass the way that lips adhere
to glass, a bit. It grins. It's pinned
apart with lab-grown cactus spines.

And drawing out this scrawl of gut
the nib is superfine, the path
is sloshed but not quite purposeless:
a rift not loaded yet with ore,
a hesitation mark to check
the ink. You blink. You breathe in deep
and scratch your name above the line.

SHELVING

The existing monuments form an ideal order.
I can see right through the ground floor sash windows
of 66–70, John Nash's first
mature commission, into Montague Street.
Cameramen were out this morning
building continuity
for Idris Elba's action flick
from nothing, from the corner of a phonebox,
filaments of plane tree streaming in the sunlight –
do the leaves come shrink-wrapped?
All I have to do today's
re-alphabetise Fiction. Two gents browse.
I know that if they've questions I can field them.
I know that when the shelves are tight
there's certain books the other books bend back to find room for.

SOCORRO

Bat twangs to beam and speeds there.
In the Langmuir Lightning Lab
a late technician clocks Socorro's
afterglow on Photoshop, a shim
between the desert and the desert
skyline, masks it with a click
and must repeat for the entire album.

Lightning pinioned
against the screen has an heraldic
lion look. (Hers is the last car
outside. Bat screams into bat.)
Who'd work with this, its bounce,
its hurled fragility, she doesn't think
but goes right through, perfecting every shot.

THE LONG 1850s

Christmas Eve the hoss
died under him it started
snowing thick he made short
shift face first inter the
yawp a toppled pine had left

down scrabbled deep dirt
shoulder-width long stretch then
broadens & he's room to breathe –
lies back pats round to
orient himself in dark

queer thing by touch it's
like he's unnaneath a bed
backweave of sackcloth
heavy mattress shifting when
he hears the knock

stays beam stiff
knock goes on like bailiff
till he twigs he's
restin broadways on the bear
ear on the bear's heart

wintering   in quarter-time
the cub he figures
unstuck from the tit
& suffocated when she
swills a real gulp of air

all restless like he
has a trick to drowsy her
he drinks deep from that tap
himself says later in that
milk he tasted *forest as a process*

May's green blister in
September's berry
shoot soil white ash
firestorm and lightning
fish and stream and portion

of the stream inside the fish
and through it
as an aftertaste
me riding and the pouch
of air I whistled with

The bear was sleepier
He yanked a root
sucked once to start the
pressure going
tied it pinch-tight round the nipple

that put her to dreaming proper
backt out found the weather
lifting and his strength
redoubled so he hefted
up the hoss onto his shoulders, walked

to where the ground was soft
enough to dig a grave
that's it about
tho an acquaintance
8 months later

passed the same spot
said the pine
had sprouted berries
big as grapes and white
he said from all the milk it suckled

THE WARREN COMMISION

'the sort of poetry Geoffrey Hill, with his customary astringency,
has labelled "home movies"'

Zapruder, when he tried to sleep
could not unfixate
on that frame

where the apricot
over the President's forehead –
how did *that* get there? –

quivered,
pulsed outward.
He dreamt of it hanging

exploded, a billboard
in Times Square,
his own

two thumbs up
like the man from Del Monte.
He dreamt that the tricky glint under the grass

had resolved itself into
a second camera,
one pointed right at him.

THE COMMON PURSUIT

Noon. Shadows draw back into their shells.
The ants whose trick it is to run on desert
ground have made the safety of their burrow

or are baked husks now; the first task
for the colony this evening will be
dragging corpses home to feed the grubs.

The grubs are burnt-up ants reincarnated.
Death has its own burrow, scurry scurry,
pinhole narrowing and narrowing until

they spill out swimming stranded in the Queen.
The nest's built on a shifty brink already;
nothing can be wasted but the drones.

Ant sisters brush antennae in the tunnels
for a small soothe, almost skim across the sand.
(The other insects have a jerky clockwork

waterboatman tread, a predawn stalk.)
By 10 a.m. the ants are all that's out.
Extravagance you might call it. Void baroque.

CANDIDATES

Now I am down in that smashed bandit valley
where among the redstone crockery
erosional protrusions
look like us, or buggy beta god-dumped goes at us.

       'And having felt for ages like a sack of spores
       I plan to get my edges back on Mars.
       The key to self-respect is contrast.'

The lake we must pretend we haven't seen
The Packard raising dust we mustn't walk towards
The moon we must imagine doubled up
The us I must bed down and never use

       GSOH. Love to cook. Travel, obviously.
       Fight for me. I enjoy a night in with a DVD.
       Immortalise me. Die for me. I like to keep fit.
       Here, I'll tie my favour to your helmet.

Hand on shoulder of the man
in front we are proceeding blind through knotty
rock crop – where the linebreaks
come the whisper goes back 'halt!' and pick ourselves around them.

       Am I wary of these new gods?
       No one has proved who put me here
       and if they'll care when I am dust.
       At least the new gods are among us.

Good old midget rattler
Right here he shucked
His spacesuit, gathered
Himself in the shadow

It's our genes speaking,
obsessed with lineage – little tyrants.
The throne must tumble through the sons.
We're just the land, we give them what they want.

Emptiness isn't empty,
it's filled with tat.
The wind pares grain from rock and whines *I hate this place*.
Noon makes a slowly clenching fist of air.

My current interests include fitness /
nutrition / hematite / my bones
brittling / how to be in the night.

Goblins or hoodoo rocks
are natural sandstone.
Mushroom, teeter-totter or executive
desk toy are the varieties they come in.

now the moon is laughably close:
curled hair on my coat
mouthful of sour breath
eye rolling through its phases in my head

What's the case for man on Mars? There is no case.
We sent up a pronghorn instead
to make up for the one which got struck by our minibus.

o cairo & dublin & austin
o moscow & trieste & rutland
o palakkad & ellisras
you couldn't keep your sons & daughters

Omniscience rerouted into Utah
Where each day the Bluffdale Reservoir
Lessens perceptibly, from cooling servers:
To the care of which, the NSA
Farms out its schlubs. I want that schlub
Tending a server clump in Bluffdale
Before the weekend, comes the edict: out
The poor schlub goes, the daughter changes school
Which is tremendously disruptive. Trapped
Careerists have it worse, though. Gossip
And small daily kindnesses sustain them,
Doubtless, through another lunch hour in Bluffdale,
Another evening falling in the canyon
Where dark falls quickly. They leave to collect
Their soccer-playing daughters. Fifteen minutes
Thinking of them and I drift into a sort of
Schlub pastoral, like *The Simpsons*.
Empson said pastoral was a subworld
Mapped precisely to the surface world, but stripped
Down, sprueless, 'as among swains or clowns',
The same way data boils down to tendency:
Paw's Google history, Maw's plumber hunt
Are noise the schlub shaves. I suppose
There's worse make-work, worse fates
Than ending up their joke or toast. Tonight
I'll think of their small talk at secret
Potluck, so-and-so's promotion, worry lingering
Round [name redacted]'s meteoric rise –
Main worry being, meteors don't rise.

DONALD DAVIE IN NASHVILLE

'However sparred or fierce
the furzy elements...' – the steel guitars
he never learnt to recognise,
Merle Haggard's voice, a bed of tinny
feedback – 'let them be but few,
and spaciously dispersed,
and excellence appears.'
His taxi to the airport
ups the volume on a gospel show.

A transplant, hating country music,
his new campus, how the students
see him as a pinko Brit
and not the brawling Tory of *PN Review*,
he takes a backward look at Music City –
neon bars, the empty megachurch. It's sparse as hell.

RAMSONDE

Every morning with his ramsonde and resistograph
he plots the snowpack's weakness as a jaggy coastline.
From that gauges chance of avalanche.

Within his quadrant he can radio roads closed,
bar skiers from the slopes, and snowshoed hikers
dawdle over coffee for his estimate.

His rifle is dismantled, reassembled, constantly.
His map too, and his sense of how the snowfalls
slot together, layer into layer.

Once, along the ridge, he felt the ground writhe
underneath his boots, and then the mountain shrugged.
He crawled out downslope, dragging home his leg.

Unchoosy about company: the bear man following
a collar's radar blip to find the den, the helicopter
ambulance he'll chat conditions with.

Responsibility is hammering the ramsonde, milled
harpoon, into the glacier's whaleback, to listen
for the sigh. The sigh flows upward through his hand.

HIGH TABLE

Unpanelling the Combination Room
they drew out through the cavity one foot,
ten feet, two hundred feet of copper wire.

Tangled in it – birdnests made of spit –
were little lacquered microphones, antique,
a dozen to be undone, tapped and rolled

across the palm, arcane beige lozenges.
They felt too close to Christmas cracker toys
to make it sordid even: all those ears

and far-off rows of secretaries typing,
the archives full of gossip, years of port
which circulated, like a rough translation.

YVOR WINTERS AND BUFFY SUMMERS

'Professor Winters, more alive
than any critic writing now to form –
and deaf to diction.' – Donald Davie.

In *Buffy* everything was utter diction.
The dialogue, champagne-
glass xylophone, made sound

each fine gradation of ironic.
Where could cadence adhere
but in diction? (In the music?

Winters had made mincemeat
of the music, when he held up
moral truth as poetry's true measure.)

     *

*In every generation
is a Chosen One, and she alone
will fight against the vampires,*

the demons, and the forces
        not of darkness
but of too much light

thrown on the personal
(an inverse Zorro
in his author photo, just the eyes

behind thick specs, the rest
a crumpled shadow);
thrown on those terms

     *

like *cadence, diction, form*
the reader grows increasingly suspicious of,
suspecting that they can't be paraphrased.

A gang of useful figments.
All his enemies would peel to ash
in daylight, never fog a mirror.

Still he had them at his nerve-endings.
Was that what scared him into criticism?
        – Ancestral memory of bodge,

the ruined prom, demons in limousines,
a worry something vital wouldn't hold,
the marquee sagging on a broken rib?

IN A DARPA LAB

Civilians still can't believe
that moth control's been field-ready
since the 90s, think of that,
when phones were corncob size

boys here could brainjack moths
and steer them through
a Coors Light bottle neck or flaming
donut hole, whatever obstacles the lab thought up that weekend.

What's the trick? Well
knocking out the input from the left
or right eye makes 'em bank the other way.
To figure pitch and yaw took longer.

You've got fifteen minutes
flight time, max., before the stem burns out.
On demo day for five-star generals
we'd lay on a dozen, let them take the throttle.

Whole goddamn moth armies!
Flaking chalk
they buzz the general's coffee.
Proof of concept, Joey, proof of concept!

FIREWATCHING

Hi-viz jacket
Through a Tavistock
Square window
Glowing slightly

Ill at ease
Its own light
Pooling underneath
The coatstand

Too much like
The decade-old
Pub candle in
The Pineapple

Each new stem
Hammered down
Into the over-
Running ones

Below, an emblem
Eliot rejected
For 'Tradition' –
It implied

A simple edge
Of flame, translucent
Yellow you
Could just make out

Black curlicues
Of spent wick through
So he was wise
To scrap it

TWO BIRDS

i.

Nothing
musses like feathers, it's sacrilegious almost
to run your finger against the grain of one
shifting barbs out of true. I remember
watching the mad swan
gouge at her back on the millpond,
her upright neck for a moment like nothing
so much as a flint in a fist then it falling.
The feathers she rose with
grew redder as she wound down in her own
spun circles. This was the Granta.
The head on my pint was still as the dusk she soaked into.
I watched bubbles hurling against it and every time failing.

ii.

In the bone three chevron dints
where lanes merge. Mass of hair and speckled fat.
The pheasant's shattered
undercarriage is its best bit, from the top
[Fig #1] it has a kohl-eyed doofus look,
tomb art or the Nubian Book of the Dead.
I like it here
where down clings on
like marram to a dune. I like the scruffiness
disclosed on grace. Poor shocked stuck thing!
Wrenching the neck – crosshatching
to finish it off – you close the sketchbook
and it rides home in the boot, on two sheets of newspaper.

GUATAVITA

To stall catastrophe
councils rounded up all disposable gods
and emptied them into the lake.

Those gold alligators –
had they been sisters in myth?
Later only converts would speak of them,

or of the one-day king
on his bark barge, raising both arms
and toppling backward

not under the weight of the sun
but the fiddly
glyph in his gut.

Conquistador linguists
work on translating
the idea of 'real, existent'

as something
a person can point at.
Most stories half check out

then trail off
into the deeper jungle,
from which an advance party

staggers occasionally, clothes
rotted onto their back and a hot scheme
for undermining some legendary mountain.

FOR THE OLD CAVENDISH LABORATORIES

All three entrances felt like the back way: omnipresent skip and bins, the discard of a permanent refurb; spent gas tanks wedging firedoors; porter's cubby, stairwells I can't reconcile to a mental map, and every sign a laminated stand-in, as if any open route was temporary, as if Crick and Watson's sandwich trolley had negotiated eerily distinct strangeways and spandrels on a scheme which made about as little sense as this one; arcane parking (why a space *there*? surely no-one's car could take that corner); rain-shadow of Arup's boosted tower – its concrete so waterlogged and friable, I heard an HB pencil could be screwed in deep enough to bite...

Underneath the floorboards was a perfect inch of mercury, six decades' spillage. They were laying lines for nitrogen. My father and John Hanlon from Estates and Buildings walked out on a joist to watch it lob their torch-beams home. John said eventually, 'We can't just leave this here.'

RAIN BIRD

When the screw thread on a plastic nozzle head
gives way, which come to think of it's
their only failure mode, I mosey over
with a satchel of replacement nozzle heads,
a square-bit key to turn the intermittent off,
a while spare to dawdle vaguely shaded, like the beans, by spritz.

The rain-bird is a sort of square-bit key
unlocking California to green.
You think about the Calaveras
crumpling behind the dam, extruded
through its pinchpoints, culverts, aqueducts
to hammer here, a thousand wings in sync, down mile latitudes.

Yessir, you think about it for a while,
wing as waterfern, as fern of water,
wing as feather, fractalling to spray
to swansdown drifting through no breeze
to gloss on leaf, the green blade of the possible.
Then you jerk the key back and start for the access road.

A BLENDED INDEX

Titles strut
in sumptuary caps,
range lordly over
the entire alphabet

as first lines mob
round *A* and *I*
and hunker down
behind [ ] barricades.

T FOR TEXAS

Every source seems to take it as read
that in those days 'brakeman' was synonym
for 'agreeable', that his yodel mimicked, lyrebird-fashion,
a trainwhistle's dip and wheel, its Doppler
ripple through gaps in the rockwall –

though now it sounds more like a trick
of the wind down an empty canyon, plaintiveness
in his voice mistaken for plain good nature.
TB in German translates as 'addiction to dwindling'.
The next train does not call at this station.

WHAT GROWS, AND SOME DIVISIONS

Space programmes / screwbean mesquite / barrel cactus
Ecoregion / section / tract

> The intricacies of a desert
> lawncare business,
> 'Quarter million a year'
> says José Luis, carefully,
> two cylinders of rolled lawn
> harnessed to his flatbed.
> I took them for lumber
> till I saw him truck them through the carwash
>
> which procedure
> so he told me
> he repeated every hundred miles.
> These were destined for a county courthouse.
> His son, tall strong boy,
> came out the restroom, vaulted to the cab

Heat creep in metal / arrowweed / salt cedar
Freeway / sightline / spitting distance

> Evening they'll
> unfurl the turf like prayermats
> over nothing earth
> prepped minimally,
> one bare step from dust.
> He showed me how the sprinkler jib
> rotated in its mechanism:
> that small click I knew
>
> from suburb walks at night in proper cities.
> Nothing could it draw from underneath
> he said, nor did the roots make purchase.

When the buyer moved out
he could roll his lawn back up
and take it with him

Mortgage payments owing / yucca / velvet mesquite
Habitat / range / territory

There was a lot of moving out
in evidence along our vector:
one after another, deathbed towns
whose rationale was irretrievable.
The stretch between
the bright spots in the web grew wider.
José Luis and his son spent more time each year
driving lawn to lawn.

They had a tanker-trailer
for the feed.
They both shook hands
goodbye, we overtook them
one gas station later. I believe
they drove almost in silence and such distances

Hard thoughts / tasajillo / sweet acacia
Boundary line / state line / horizon

THE SIGNAL AND THE NOISE

Frostbite starts
as numb song from the palm,
the lowest note left thrumming in a bellrope.

By the time
it reaches the attention
fingertips have swum outside your orbit.

Antsy void
where every sense but vision's
blared with signal: in the white, distractions

amplify
and newfound fistlessness
is one more datum. You lose purchase

on the edges
of your focus first. Then
one by one the other outposts blink blank.

REVALUATION

As Cornford runs out
pop the sniper scoops him up
and sets him down,
like rearranging something on a mantelpiece.

Córdoba glows blue.
HQ is a radio receiver
trollied with great sweat and thumps
to where the fighting's thinnest.

    *

No news back in Cambridge.
Bookshop gossip
puts him in Sierra Guadalupe.
One clearout later

(useless till receipts, an invoice
seven years past due, box
after box of Stalinalia, unsaleable)
two ms. poems left behind the counter for safekeeping disappear.

    *

Across town, Leavis
marks up galley proofs for his
Revaluation (not, you understand, that he
has changed his mind on anything –

'revaluation' means the reader's job).
The study lightbulb goes   and hangs there,
absolutely still, while Leavis on a chair
unscrews instead the world from round the lightbulb.

Holy Toledo! Bill King hollered from the Raiders' dugout,
Stabler fumbled, Casper had recovered in the endzone:

> and we are here as on a darkling plain
> swept with a sudden confused calm –
> as though the airhorns all inhaled simultaneously –
> where, below us, floodlit knuckleheads
> collide, *Holy Toledo!*, and the field goal
> falls out of nowhere in the final seconds.

PEACH TREE

for Jack Baker

Things grow around particularities,
a footpath doglegged at a field boundary,
a feral peach conniving with the angle
of a roof to funnel sunlight
through its leaves and pericarp.
Jack said that certain poems
could bend thought like that,
'The Auroras of Autumn' he mentioned.

We can be sure that no-one
reads a poem Rilke's way,
now change your life, bam,
now, presumably, change it again.
You'd never get through an anthology.
Really to read properly is to buzz low over
our future lives in a cropduster,
throwing out stumbling blocks.

NOTES

Quotations, even in quotation marks, are freehand and cavalier.

'From the Journals of Don Diego de Vargas' is a found poem. This entry is dated December 18th 1692. My version draws heavily on the literal translation by L. Bradford Prince, included in *Spanish Mission Churches of New Mexico* (Iowa: Torch Press, 1915).

The translation of Ibn Hamdis (1056?–1133) is by Herbert Howarth and Ibrahim Shakrullah, in *Images from the Arab World* (London: Pilot Press, 1944).

The right-justified verse paragraphs of 'Candidates' are by Rachel Piercey.

That Donald Davie never learnt to recognise a steel guitar is surely belied by his own 'Nashville Mornings' ('Damnable steel guitar'), but he said so himself in a letter to Gareth Reeves, which I have been shown. The quotation is from Davie's 'Ezra Pound in Pisa'.

The second of the 'Two Birds' is from a picture by Claire Williams.

ACKNOWLEDGEMENTS

Thanks are due to the editors of the following journals and publications in which some of these poems have previously appeared: *PN Review*, *Poetry Review*, *Magma*, *The White Review*, *The Rialto*, *Sunday Times*, *Oxford Poetry*, *London Review of Books*, *New Poetries VI* (Carcanet, 2015), *Best British Poetry 2014* (Salt, 2014).

I am grateful to Jack Baker, James Brookes, John Canfield, Joey Connolly, Rishi Dastidar, Patrick Davidson Roberts, Katy Evans-Bush, Emily Hasler, Holly Hopkins, Amy Key, Chris Larkin, Roddy Lumsden, Alex Macdonald, Rachel Piercey, Gareth Reeves, Declan Ryan, Martha Sprackland, Joe Williams, and Emma Wright, for advice and encouragement.

Special thanks to Eleanor Lischka for her assistance with the Spanish, to Oscar Barlow and Carmen Rohsmann-Sinnott, to Alice Mullen, to Sarah Clegg (for her help in lesson #3), and to Annick Sawala, who has not forsaken me yet.